Journey to Release
Counselling in a UK Prison

Mo Smith

With the assistance of Toni Close

⩲ WATERSIDE PRESS

Journey to Release: Counselling in a UK Prison
Mo Smith
With the assistance of Toni Close

ISBN 978-1-909976-49-8 (Paperback)
ISBN 978-1-910979-43-3 (Epub ebook)
ISBN 978-1-910979-44-0 (Adobe ebook)

Cataloguing-In-Publication Data A catalogue record for this book can be obtained from the British Library.

e-book *Journey to Release: Counselling in a UK Prison* is available as an ebook and also to subscribers of Ebrary, Ebsco, Myilibrary and Dawsonera.

Printed by Lightning Source

Main UK distributor Gardners Books, 1 Whittle Drive, Eastbourne, East Sussex, BN23 6QH. Tel: +44 (0)1323 521777; sales@gardners.com; www.gardners.com

USA and Canada distributor Ingram Book Company, One Ingram Blvd, La Vergne, TN 37086, USA. (800) 937-8000, orders@ingrambook.com, ipage.ingrambook.com

Published 2017 by
Waterside Press Ltd., Sherfield Gables, Sherfield on Loddon, Hook, Hampshire
United Kingdom RG27 0JG
Telephone +44(0)1256 882250
Email enquiries@watersidepress.co.uk
Online catalogue WatersidePress.co.uk

Table of Contents

About the authors

Mo Smith is a senior accredited counsellor and supervisor, and a Fellow of the Counselling in Prisons Network. In addition to working at HMP X, she has a successful private practice. She is also a qualified teacher.

Toni Close is a writer of fiction and non-fiction. She has a Master's degree in Occupational Psychology and a background in teaching and publishing.

Together they have also co-authored *The Cinnabar Toolkit for Counsellors, Volume 1*, Therapy Professional Press, 2016.

Acknowledgements

I would like to acknowledge the tremendous support I receive from Jo, who takes the task of administration of the service in her stride and keeps me on my toes. Without her dedicated support, life would be so confusing.

To my daughter Toni, who has supported me in my work in the prison and in our venture, Cinnabar Training. She has taken my words and feelings and put them back together in a way that has made this book a wonderful memoir of my life in HMP X.

Also, my husband Phil who has supported my work in the prison and encouraged me throughout our years together, in everything I have achieved.

Mo Smith
July 2017

The prison

HMP X (name withheld) is a Category C prison in the UK currently holding over 800 male prisoners.

Forewords by the Governors

Neil Thomas, Prison Governor

Journey to Release stands as a hugely informative work on the important role that counselling services play in UK Prisons. It is of use to those that have an interest in counselling in general but most importantly encourages all of us in society to look beyond the word 'criminal' and see the human being underneath.

The men in our custody and care often have the inability to understand their own thoughts and emotions. When insight is gained they often struggle to communicate their feelings effectively. This lack of insight and inability to express themselves can manifest itself in a loss of control, this behaviour is often a continuous factor in their offending.

By helping prisoners to understand and express their underlying issues, Mo and her team at HMP X are playing a pivotal role in protecting the public and breaking the cycle of crime.

Michael Wood, Former Governor

Throughout my 42-year career in the Prison Service, I have had the experience of working with counselling services for both prisoners and staff and have come to respect greatly their professionalism and effectiveness.

Reducing re-offending and rehabilitating prisoners is a key priority within the Prison Service.

To this end, the service has a range of activities, interventions, strategies and pathways aimed at addressing some of the most prevalent factors influencing the life choices and attitudes of the prisoners. However, this can be difficult — or even impossible — when they are unwilling to engage with us and to try to understand the regime.

In addition, many of those in our care have a range of disorders and major risk factors in their past. Many have experienced various psychological, social, biological, cultural and environmental factors such as conflict, disaster, violence, abuse, bereavement and isolation.

We assess the needs of the prisoners in our care and identify the key work we need to do to help reduce risk and protect the public. One of the pathways we work with is linked to health, and in particular mental health—which is where counselling comes in.

During my latest Governing role, I supported the development of an internal counselling service—a service that is directly funded by the prison. By providing training opportunities for new counsellors and interesting voluntary work for experienced counsellors we were able to run it at minimal cost.

I have a firm belief that there is a need to have quality counselling services within our prisons and I have seen for myself their value, and their importance.

Counselling supports individuals who may be in crisis or at risk of self-harm or suicide and supports a decent, safe and secure living and operational environment within the prison itself.

This service gave me a good level of assurance and clearly helped me to supply very much needed support to prisoners. It also helped to support and prepare prisoners to engage with their sentence plan in order to reduce their offending and be able to successfully rehabilitate within society on release.

The Counselling Service at HMP X was something I was very proud of while I was Governor. This book tells you all about it.

"The challenges facing prisoners are multiple and can feel overwhelming at times for the therapist. However, I have felt very inspired by my encounters with prisoners — the human journey. It is resilience in the face of extreme adversity that really comes through when working in a prison environment."

A Counsellor

Cooperate
Obliging
Understanding
Neutral
Self-Respect
Emotional
Listener
Liberate
Open-Minded
Resolve

From a Client

This book is dedicated to all the prisoners who come to the Counselling Service with brave and difficult questions and share their innermost thoughts and feelings.

And to the Trainees and Counsellors who give their time freely to help them seek brave and difficult answers.

Also to the hard-working officers, staff and Governors of HMP X for supporting the service.

Introduction

The path to releasing pent up emotions and thoughts can be a painful one for anyone: locked-in feelings such as anger or frustration may have their roots in traumas that are still raw despite the passage of time.

For the prisoner, this pain can be additionally intense and impossible to escape.

As counsellors, we uncover painful events and the feelings that go with them by slowly exposing each onion-like layer. The traumas that are unearthed may include things that the client experienced through no fault of their own, or may be about decisions and actions they took because they knew no better at the time.

These events and emotions have often been living within a client for years—perhaps decades—and will have taken a toll upon them. In the prison population, pain and hurt is manifested through aches and pains, irritability and anger, an inability to relax, and a difficulty forming relationships.

In addition, the natural defence mechanisms which act to protect the psyche from unwelcome feelings can develop from light boundaries to thick impenetrable walls. These walls shut out not only the painful emotions and memories, but also everyone and everything that may be able to help, in an ironic reflection of the prison walls themselves.

HMP X (name withheld) is a Category C prison in the UK currently holding over 800 male prisoners.

In 2000, I (Mo Smith) joined HMP X's Counselling Service as a volunteer counsellor. The service was informal, but clearly doing amazing work with prisoners who wanted to engage and change.

In 2004, I became the co-ordinator of the service and began working with the Governor to introduce safer practices, develop an ethical framework, and grow the service steadily year-on-year.

HMP X's Counselling Service is unusual in the UK as it is an embedded department within the prison, independent from Healthcare and Psychology.

In other prisons, they perhaps have Cruse Bereavement agency coming in or maybe Rape Crisis in women's prisons. Some have therapy units which offer holistic treatment.

The Counselling Service deals with anything and everything: abuse, bereavement, relationships, self-harm, depression, anxiety and many more.

My job involves assessing and arranging counselling for suitable prisoners, as well as recruiting and supervising volunteer counsellors. It has been the most rewarding and fulfilling work of my life.

This book contains my thoughts and opinions about how this service works, and why. I don't pretend to know everything, but I do hope that it may be useful to others considering work in a secure setting or involved in setting-up or running a similar type of counselling service.

Along the way, I have described aspects of clients' stories with their permission and told their stories in disguise, to protect them.

"I didn't know what to expect. It was very emotional, but I now realise who I am and do not want to have anything to do with who I was."

A Client

One

Why Counsel in Prison?

Some people might ask if we should bother counselling prisoners. There is an idea, I think, that they are less than human and should be denied what are thought of as "human comforts."

To me, every prisoner who asks for counselling is a client. They are human, frail and desperate for answers to the questions of their lives. If you have a problem outside you can get help from various agencies, doctors and support workers. Why not inside prison?

Over the years, I have found that the majority of clients in the prison have experienced some form of negative situation in their childhood which can be identified as a contributing factor to their crimes.

We learn from the moment we are born: how to laugh, when to cry, how to make friends, and how to control and express our emotions. If we are not taught what is right or wrong, and how to problem-solve with compassion and empathy, how do we know what we "should" do?

We all make mistakes — some, truly awful in their scope and impact — but we are capable of regret or remorse. How many times have you said to yourself: "If only I had handled that differently" or "If only I could hold my temper"?

These are normal feelings. Prisoners experience them too. They too can say "If only" and mean it.

> "If only I had dealt with my anger when I was younger instead of waiting until now. At 48, what chance do I have of people believing that I have changed?"
>
> *A Client*

The prisoners at HMP X can work through a victim awareness course to gain an understanding of the impact of their crime. We have had many referrals from the course (mentioned in *Chapter Four*) as this opens the client up to acknowledge what they have done.

The prisoners who request counselling are usually very remorseful about what they have done. I can't speak for the other prisoners, the ones we don't see.

When our clients come to us, they feel that their whole life has come to a standstill. They feel scarred by what they've done. Their families have often disowned them and these men feel forgotten.

At its simplest, counselling helps them to take responsibility for their crimes, and develop some impulse control to stop, think, and walk away.

> A was pushed by another prisoner again-and-again. He used all the self-control that his counsellor had helped him find.
>
> "I'm not going to hit you, I am going to walk away and I suggest you do too," he said.

An officer saw this exchange. He found me and told me what had happened. He told me that A had changed dramatically from the angry man who had arrived at the prison.

B came to counselling wanting answers. Four years ago, he had beaten his three-year-old daughter to death.

Now, still living inside the cloud of shock that had descended on him that night, he asked: "Why did I do it?" and "What on earth was I thinking?"

He said: "My life is over — I deserve everything that is happening to me."

I always give the counsellors the opportunity to decline a client. In this case, one of the counsellors said that she needed to do so because her own daughter would be on her mind. The counsellors always have this choice.

Exploring the circumstances of his crime and his life was hard for the experienced prison counsellor eventually assigned to B. We worked together during supervision, talking about the memories from her own past that were stirred by her sessions with him and making sure that boundaries were maintained. The counsellor worked on her issues in her own personal therapy and kept in touch with me regularly. They moved forward.

B had been abandoned by his mother when he was five-years-old and left to live with a strict aunt and uncle. He was beaten with a belt regularly and locked away without food or water.

When he became a young man he escaped, only to find himself in an alleyway one night, beaten and sexually assaulted.

That was when he decided to fight back against a world that was his enemy. Alcohol became his friend — the only thing that could wipe out his memories. His relationships were abusive and he often lost control.

One night, his partner said the wrong thing, rejecting him. He beat her and then set upon the screaming child.

The guilt and shame B brought to his sessions was huge. Counselling didn't — couldn't — wipe away his feelings or what he had done, but it enabled him to understand the chain of events and connections that had led him to that terrible night and to begin to accept his actions.

During the times he was locked away by his aunt and uncle, B had learned to bury his feelings. Counselling helped him to access them, and acknowledge the pain and hurt his inner-child was still suffering. He managed to write a letter to that inner-child, apologising to himself for the choices he had made and the path he had taken.

B had a long road to travel. He was not going to be able to forgive himself for what he had done, but gradually he decided that he wasn't going to take his life.

The counsellor who saw B grew as a professional herself during the work. I feel that it is important to allow counsellors to develop at their own pace and only see the most challenging clients when they are ready and in a stable place.

C had been harming himself for years, driven by feelings from his childhood and the inner-voice of a judgemental father.

When he came to prison, he finally received the help he needed to stop harming and move forward.

He walked into the room, sat down and exhaled deeply.

I said, "That sounded like relief?"

He smiled a little grimly and told me he had been wanting to talk to a counsellor for many years but that none of the prisons he had been in had been able to provide the service.

C told me that he had been put into care from birth, moving from foster home to foster home until he had been taken in by a loving family when he was five.

Tragically, his new parents were killed in a road accident and he was put into a care home.

He remembered the loss vividly — his earliest memories were of disappointment, confusion, loss and sadness.

C was an angry boy who grew into an angry man and got into lots of fights. He was always in trouble. Behind the challenging and demanding little boy was a secret story of abuse in the care home. When he tried to tell, he was beaten and sexually assaulted.

No-one listened to him. When he ran away, he was brought back.

This beginning taught him that he was valueless, pointless, unwanted and unworthy.

In despair, he tried to kill himself. Ironically, drugs saved his life, giving him another way to cope — to escape his life.

C worked hard and showed me that he valued his session by always being on time and making sure that he was showered and tidy for me (this is an important measure of respect in prison as it is easy to let things go).

Soon he decided that he wanted to go to the police — to stand up for himself against the system and people who had abused him. This only became possible because of the work we did in our sessions–building his self-worth and replacing his little-boy understanding with an adult's insight.

He felt that — as a boy — his care home abusers and foster carers had taught him to get angry and lash out. The man he was becoming during our sessions understood that he was responsible for his own actions now, and that those actions could bring him back to prison.

C also began to believe that he could be a good husband, lover and father. To do this, he would have to work hard to change his instinct that fighting was the answer.

After coming to terms with what had happened to him in the care home, he realised he needed to act to ensure that the people who had abused him were punished. He felt uncomfortable with the thought that they might have "helped" other children — or might still be carers.

I sat with him in silence while he made his statement to the police.

C got his day in court, and eventually those responsible for the widespread abuse at that care home were found guilty.

He then wanted to help others "on the out" (slang for after release).

We discussed who he wanted to help and how. We talked about the consequences of telling his story for himself and for the family he had now, the stigma of letting people know that he had been in prison, and the potentially strong emotions of those touched and affected by his story of abuse.

When he felt ready, he set about finding ways that he could share his story at schools and self-help groups. He sourced agencies that he could approach, and courses he could attend at college.

His goal? To help kids understand that drugs and crime are not the answer.

I am sure that most of the clients I have seen in HMP X over the years have shown some level of personal growth because of their sessions.

The clients feel supported at a time when they wonder if everyone has given up on them. Some of them have never had one-to-one attention, or someone who will help them find their own answers.

Many clients have said to me: "I don't want to come back to prison." I find they are very motivated to change their behaviour. After counselling—and realising in some cases that life is too short and they want a future—they are even more motivated to try and change their lives, turn them around.

Sometimes families tell them "enough is enough." They are no longer welcome in their homes because of their crimes. This is also good motivation for change.

I can't provide evidence that those prisoners who received counselling were less likely to re-offend when they left prison, or that their lives and relationships had been improved.

The logistics of prison are complicated. Prisoners can be transferred to other prisons many miles away with little or no notice, or a parole hearing can result in their release. In either case, it is difficult to follow their story and collect information on subsequent behaviour.

There are also so many other factors that might affect the behaviour of prisoners upon release, such as the availability of support and guidance on the outside and a safe place to stay.

D appeared to have things under control when he got out of prison. He had a job and a place to live. He was working hard and wanted to do well.

Then, one night his brother was drawn into a fight. He was badly injured and died.

D was distraught.

When he bumped into the man who had killed his brother during an ordinary night out, he reacted. All his self-control fell away, and he found himself back in prison again.

I was walking down a corridor in the prison when D came up to me and said, "I'm sorry."

"What do you mean?" I said.

"I let you down," he said, his voice full of emotion.

I told him that he hadn't let me down. Something had happened that he hadn't been prepared for. It is what it is.

Some weeks later, D came back to counselling and we started again with the hope that this time he could find that elusive control that would make this his last time in prison.

I believe wholeheartedly that counselling has a positive impact on a person's ability to overcome their past, to accept themselves, and to understand others. Prisoners are no different in that respect.

Comments from Colleagues

"The Counselling Service has been provided to the residents of HMP X for a number of years. This service has helped a great number of the men with complex issues to access help, support and guidance during difficult times in their sentences.

It is important to note that without this service the men in our care would continue to experience their current thoughts and behaviours. Without the support of the counselling services provided the men would not be able to deal with their own, often painful issues which in some cases result in blockers to addressing their offending and prevent re-integration into the community.

The counselling team are a positive addition to the running of a large establishment. On behalf of the men and staff within HMP X, I want to thank Mo and her team for the ongoing support over a number years and hope that this will continue going forward."

Adam Megicks, Governor, Head of Residence and Safety

"The Counselling Service is a small service with a big impact.

Counselling helps individuals explore the reasons why they offend and is a vital step to reduce their re-offending.

The service runs on a volunteer basis with only a very small amount of funding the counsellors working in their own time to provide the vital steps to help pave the way for individuals to make changes.

There is a definite need for this service and the waiting list only proves how many are willing to embrace the support so that they can move forward."

Julie Martin, Head of Safer Prisons and Equalities

All prisoners have a probation officer on the outside. Inside, they have an offender manager (OM) who manages the prisoner's sentence, ensures courses are completed, and coordinates with other departments. Our Counselling Service is constantly in touch with the OMs for reports for parole.

"I feel counselling is very worthwhile whilst prisoners are in custody as for some it is the first time that they have been able to address longstanding issues. For some, their issues are linked to offending and why they behave and react to situations in the same way constantly.

It helps when prisoners are in crisis and I am not qualified to take on their issues. But, realising they have issues that need addressing and then directing them to counsellors, they are able to gain better coping skills given to them by trained professionals."

Offender Manager

"I consider the Counselling Service to be invaluable in my role. I think it is beneficial to offenders who wish to take stock of their lives, essentially confronting uncomfortable and often painful issues which other offending behaviour work does not address. This in my opinion does help in reducing reoffending."

Offender Supervisor

Chapter Summary: *Why Counsel in Prison?*

- Counselling helps to release trauma that is trapped inside prisoners.

- Counselling can help to reduce re-offending.

- More data needs to be collected to inform best practice.

"Counselling ... made me grow up."

A Client

Two

Safeguards

When the service began in 2000, it had few safeguards and was run entirely from an officer's notebook.

Anyone who wanted to refer a prisoner to a counsellor contacted the officer who made a note in the book (in his free time), and then allocated the next available client to the next available volunteer counsellor.

The volunteers came to the prison armed with three pieces of information: a name, a prison number, and a wing. They arrived at reception and were then escorted throughout the prison by officers, who waited outside the counselling room while they saw their clients.

There was no security vetting, recruitment process, notes of sessions, records of volunteers or supervision. Prisoners were allocated randomly, and there was no follow-up or support if issues were raised during sessions.

The officer who ran the service did the best he could and he believed in the work of providing counselling to prisoners. He didn't have the time or the framework though to ensure that it was done ethically and effectively.

Perhaps the most frustrating outcome was that occasionally the counsellors couldn't cope with aspects of the client's story and counselling was ended. The prisoner was left feeling uncertain and abandoned; and the counsellor moved on without addressing the underlying issues in supervision.

In 2004, the officer moved on after doing a great job of holding the fledgling service together.

At that point, I received full support from the Governor to set up whatever was needed.

Counsellors who are interested in joining the team at the prison are now required to fill in an application form. This enables me to check whether they have insurance, see where they are in their studies, and find out why they wanted to come into the prison and if they had any experience in secure settings.

Successful applicants then go through a security vetting process and attend the prison induction. They are issued keys and told how to work safely in the prison — just like any other employee.

The process underlines the seriousness of the setting. Counsellors are told about what would happen if they were to be involved in a disturbance in the prison, and they sign the Official Secrets Act.

Once the counsellor has passed through the prison's processes, they then have to agree to abide by a Code of Ethics which outlines what is expected of them professionally as a counsellor in the service. This includes confidentiality and fitness to practice, and provides a framework for managing conflicts.

Counsellors are also instructed to keep detailed notes of every session and every client they see while in this placement. Revelations of child abuse are frequent and notes can protect the counsellor and aid the client in any future court actions.

It is the responsibility of the counsellor to keep their notes secure during their tenure with the client. After their final session, the notes are transferred to the prison and archived.

Counsellors are not allowed to keep copies of their notes, but—if the client consents—they may use their stories for case studies once the names have been disguised.

As part of their placement, counsellors also agree to have an appropriate amount of supervision with me, depending on the number of client hours they accrue.

Originally, volunteers could choose any supervisor, often selecting the person who they saw for their other client work. However, the prison identified potential security concerns in allowing volunteers to discuss prisoners' stories and provide information about conditions and procedures within the prison to outside parties who had not been security vetted, and had not signed the Official Secrets Act.

Also, it was hard to find a supervisor who could understand the unique way of life inside a prison, and the types of crimes we were hearing about.

In 2005, the prison asked me to become qualified to supervise the volunteers myself. I gained a diploma and then became an accredited supervisor. Now, all counsellors at the prison must receive supervision from me, keeping the process in-house.

The supervision that volunteers receive from me is similar to the supervision that would accompany private work, but

I have a more pronounced responsibility for the security of the prison, the welfare of the clients, and the ethical and safe conduct of the counsellors.

Supervision is critical in the counselling service. I insist on absolute honesty from the counsellors. I aim to provide a non-judgmental space for them to bring anything to me. Occasionally a new or inexperienced counsellor will try to keep something back, but I am clear with them that, in the prison, this can sometimes have terrible consequences. If a counsellor has been approached and asked to contact someone on the outside, for example, or if they have become aware that their client is taking drugs, then they have to pass that information to me. Failure to do so contravenes our Code of Ethics and can lead to real harm befalling their client. The prisoners are vulnerable adults, and the risk of self-harm, suicide, and aggression is always present.

In addition to supervision, the counsellors are required to attend a every three months. At these meetings we discuss any security issues in the prison and other news relating to the Counselling Service. Counsellors are also encouraged to discuss their experiences in the prison. This helps us all to see how others work and everyone has the opportunity to share their ideas. It is important for us all to get together regularly and I feel it bonds us and makes us a team.

Since the service has developed, there is more structure for the client, and expectations on both sides are now managed. Clients know when the counsellor is due to see them and agree to a contract outlining the scope of the sessions and their commitment to the process. The principles of confidentiality are agreed, including the exceptions relating to substance use and potential for harm that are specific to the prison setting. Clients also understand that eligibility for counselling is linked to good behaviour.

Feedback from the client is important for us. At the end of their final session, clients are given a questionnaire that they can return directly to me. In it, they are asked for their views about the counselling they experienced and to iden- tify whether they have seen an improvement in areas such as physical pain and stress. Results are collated every year for the Governor.

Support for the service is provided by an administrative team who carry out daily management tasks and provide a presence for the volunteers to go to if they have any problems or questions. This team runs the booking system and deals with enquiries or complaints, as well as putting the volunteers through their vetting and inductions.

The service provided by this team has grown tremendously in the last few years, with more and more responsibility for ensuring best practice and supporting the volunteers.

Chapter Summary: *Safeguards*

- The Counselling Service at HMP X has changed considerably over the years.

- There is now a rigourous recruitment and induction process for all would-be volunteers.

- Detailed and accurate notes are imperative to safeguard counsellors and their clients.

"Working in this environment challenges me — every week that I am there."

A Counsellor

Three

Providing a Service

The counselling process within HMP X was created with two main concerns at heart: to have clear boundaries, to ensure the safety of both counsellor and client; and to assure confidentiality (within limits) so that there could be trust.

First, counselling is considered in the sentence planning report when a prisoner arrives at the prison and the service is introduced to them by Offender Management.

The process begins with a referral system. Prisoners can self-refer by filling in a form or asking a member of staff to fill one in for them, or they can be referred through their work, Healthcare, Education, chaplaincy or wing staff. Anyone who feels it may be beneficial can talk to the prisoner about the service, and fill in a referral form with the prisoner's approval.

The referral is an important first step — it marks the realisation that help is needed, and is a positive step toward change.

Some prisoners have been waiting a long time for the opportunity to talk to someone; others are only just realising that they have a problem and make use of the resources that HMP X has made available.

Sometimes prisoners have long sentences and their request for counselling comes at the very beginning. I often ask them to work on some issues and come back after they have spent some time in the prison. We have many clients who come back into the system.

Once their request is received, the Medical Department, Mental Health Service and Security personnel are then given the opportunity to identify any reason why they think that counselling is not a good option for this person.

This might be because they are in the early days of recovery from drug addiction, or because they have been involved in fighting on the wing, have taken hostages or threatened someone. If prisoners have misbehaved or had "nickings", then I ask them to take some time and re-apply when they feel in a more stable place.

E came up to me in the corridor. "You're a counsellor, aren't you?"

"Yes," I said.

"My parents always told me never to talk to anyone," he said. "To keep your business to yourself."

He went on to tell me that he had always followed his parents' advice but that now he had a problem and didn't know what to do.

I asked E for his name and his wing and I told him that I would meet him back there in half-an-hour to talk about the Counselling Service.

I found out that he had a bad record and Security was not keen on him being seen. I reached a compromise with them based on my assessment that E's behaviour would benefit from our sessions.

I arranged to see him with an officer outside the door. He talked and talked, and there were some awful secrets that he had been carrying around with him for a very long time.

The officer was outside the door for three more sessions. After that, E had improved his behaviour so much that the risk had been lifted. He eventually became a mentor for others and subsequently left to go to a lower category prison.

Many of the prisoners are on medication (including anti-depressants and other psychiatric drugs) and have mental health disorders. Their ability to commit to the counselling process is assessed, but there is usually no problem.

Once the prisoner is accepted for counselling, an initial assessment interview is used to discover all the current issues and challenges facing the client as well as historical and background information.

This session is designed to gather information not explore the issues as it may be some weeks before they have their first session with their counsellor. Opening them up to discuss their trauma—no matter how briefly—would leave them vulnerable.

I have heard many different stories from clients over the years during these assessments, but one factor appears most often: a problem with the way they learned to make relationships as a child by communicating and trusting others.

Some prisoners come to their first session before it becomes apparent that counselling is not right for them.

For some, it's because they think they can come and chat to a counsellor to make up for the fact that they have no family or friends. These prisoners certainly need support, but not counselling.

F came to counselling to talk about his relationships — how he could have made them better and why he had problems sustaining them.

At his first session, he froze. He wasn't ready. We agreed that he would wait and maybe come back some time in the future.

Six months later, he said he wanted to come back to counselling. He admitted that he had been abused and said he needed to talk about it.

Once he had made that admission, he was positive and motivated to talk.

After the initial assessment session, the client is then matched to a counsellor.

This process considers the counsellor's experience and personal qualities, and my understanding of his or her limits and influences in their lives that might affect their ability to cope with the issues that the client will bring to his sessions along with his personality, pace and motivation.

Much of this is indicated by their experience in other settings, the number of client hours they have worked (not including student hours), and their personal issues and perspective.

When the counsellor first sees a new client, they begin by agreeing the contract and setting out the time boundaries — clients are offered eight sessions initially. This can be extended if appropriate, although most work is done in this time.

Confidentiality is then discussed. Everything disclosed by the client is held in confidence unless it is regarding something that is life threatening to the client or another prisoner, or which contravenes another rule, such as whether drugs are being taken or obtained or "hooch" alcohol is being made.

If the client is aware of any harm posed to children, this needs to be reported straightaway.

The clients in the prison have less expectation of confidentiality than clients in other counselling settings. The prison environment requires these rules in order to keep everyone safe. The clients understand that.

I have never found this to be a problem. If a client has divulged something which may affect the security of the prison, I have told them that I will pass the information on.

Often, they have responded: "I know you have to tell, and that's okay."

The clients know that I try to be as discreet as I can.

During the sessions, counsellors are on the lookout for thoughts of suicide, giving up, not wanting to carry-on. There are precautions available to monitor clients who might be in trouble, and a process to place them under special care.

Our relationship with the officers is invaluable. They sometimes know more about the client than we can see in a counselling setting, and can identify out-of-character behaviour or worrisome moods and signs of depression.

Self-harm is everywhere. Prisoners scratch themselves, bite themselves, and even pull their hair out.

When prisoners harm themselves they are given medical treatment and then placed on a special status using a document called an ACCT (Assessment, Care in Custody and Teamwork). This document involves input from departments across the prison, outlining care that can be given to the prisoner.

The reasons why they harmed themselves often remain hidden until later, when the prisoner talks to someone. This might be someone from Healthcare, one of our counsellors or a chaplain.

> G had harmed himself so badly he had to have bandages on his arms to stop him doing it again.
>
> When we started work he was very quiet and I felt he was eyeing me up. He wasn't sure whether he could trust me or if this would be another pointless chat with a "goody, goody."
>
> I talked about neutral things at first, and then moved on to discuss his family and children. Then the tears came.
>
> G started to unload some horrific things that had happened to him in his past. As I listened, he took the blame for everything bad that had happened to him.
>
> "It was my fault," he said.
>
> "How can it be?" I asked him. "You were only three-years-old."

We worked hard to put G's abuse in perspective: an adult abuser and a small child—who had the power?

G had to forgive himself before he could stop punishing his skin.

In the prison, there is always a story behind self-harm. The guilt and shame that consumes some of the prisoners drives them to punish themselves over and over again.

A concern in the prison is that prisoners can become dependent on their contact with their counsellor. The prison is a difficult, impersonal environment and so being able to sit down and talk with a stranger can become a lifeline in their week.

Newly qualified or inexperienced counsellors can find it particularly hard to identify and accept the subtle manipulation that a lonely prisoner can express and I am reluctant to take these counsellors on unless they have some experience in a related role or another secure setting.

We use a contract to make the boundaries of the relationship as clear as possible, and I monitor counsellors during supervision for signs that boundaries might be slipping or signs that they might be inadvertently colluding with their client.

An important boundary in any counselling relationship is the ending of that relationship. In the prison, this must be carefully managed so that prisoners don't feel abandoned.

If all is going well, the client will be reminded during Session Five that their agreed contract specified eight sessions in total. If there is more work to do, extensions may be made and the contract is renegotiated with the client.

Occasionally a client will want to see their counsellor after they are released. Counsellors are told to refuse this absolutely. Instead, they can refer their client to another counsellor or agency in the geographical area of their release, or talk to their probation officer who may be able to help.

At every stage the client is given the information they need so they know where they stand and can make their own decisions to continue or not.

At the end, I try to ensure that the client is empowered to say, "I've done what I wanted to." This doesn't always happen. Sometimes, the wider machinery of the prison system intrudes.

> H had been in counselling for an extended number of sessions and was working very well on childhood issues that had provoked his anger and his crime.
>
> One day I walked in to be told that he was gone. He had been transferred to a different prison.

I felt abandoned (a feeling that I took to my supervisor in our next session), but I was also concerned that he would feel that his good work was now gone, and the experience of counselling had been pointless — all because the process had been terminated without warning.

I later found out that he had chosen to continue working on himself and had been able to arrange counselling with an outside agency at his new prison.

We work to the principle that a client can leave at any time either through a transfer to another prison, or if their parole is granted. If they have been in counselling for a while, I do what I can to request a hold on transfers; failing that I try to contact the transfer prison and see if there is someone there who can continue where we leave off.

> J had been in counselling, talking about his sexual abuse when his transfer notice to a less secure prison came through. He chose to defer the move until he had reached a suitable ending point and could consolidate the work he had done with his counsellor.

Occasionally, the client will ask for a record of their counselling to go to their offender manager to be considered at their parole hearing.

I write a short report, make sure the prisoner is comfortable with its contents, and then send it for inclusion with their parole documents. In these reports, I can comment on their motivation and commitment to the process, and their remorse or insight into their crime.

When K first came to prison, he was angry and always "a bother" to the staff. Three years into a nine-year sentence, he applied for counselling. He wouldn't say why. On his form, he simply wrote that he would only tell a counsellor.

Security initially rejected his application for counselling because of his behaviour. They told him that they would reconsider their recommendation if he could stay out of trouble for two weeks.

Two weeks later we began.

K told me that his grandfather had taught him to fight and stand up for himself, beating him when he showed signs of being afraid as a young boy. Since those early lessons, he had been in trouble for most of his life and had upset most of the people in his life.

I found out that K didn't have a good relationship with the officers. On the wing, he was nicknamed "Waste of Space."

Half way through our session he stopped talking. Silence fell.

I asked him what he was thinking.

He told me that he hated fighting, but couldn't tell anyone. He thought the other prisoners would take advantage of him if they knew. We explored his feelings toward his grandfather and the anger and fear that fuelled his fighting.

Toward the end of our sessions, I was asked to write a parole report. I was able to write about K's motivation to change. When I showed the report to him, he became emotional and thanked me for seeing the real man within.

Every day we work alongside Healthcare, Mental Health and the other departments in the prison. The Psychology Department also ask sometimes for our input on the motivation and commitment of a prisoner.

It is a group effort to give these men as much support as we can.

Chapter Summary: *Providing a Service*

- The service begins with a referral system that any prisoner or staff member can access.

- Confidentiality is essential, but has necessary limits.

- Transfers can be sudden and so counsellors have to make every session count.

"Counselling really helped me see my life; it was scary but very worthwhile."

A Client

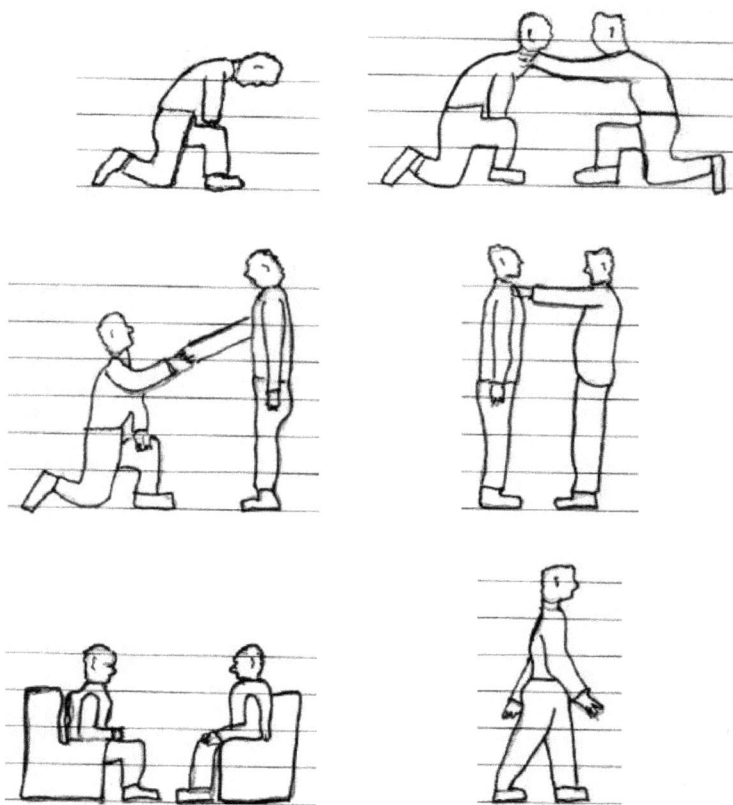

A client's view of counselling

Four

Our Clients

We use interview rooms for counselling. They are stark rooms at first glance, but the chairs are comfortable and the window lets in the sunlight. We have an alarm button on the wall and a whistle that we can use to call for assistance.

There are no decorations or accessories like lamps or tables, but our clients are not looking for a warm cosy space — they arrive with single-minded focus on their need. The walls just fall away.

Clients in prison are incredibly varied in their ages, cultures, religions, and beliefs; but nearly all come into counselling to talk.

Some prisoners work hard and are really motivated; some take the time to understand and engage with the counselling process. Sometimes it's about their journey to find answers: Why did this happen? Why did I do it? Why?

The prisoners at HMP X have been sentenced for a variety of crimes with four years or more still to serve. Crimes include burglary, fraud, GBH (grievous bodily harm), assault, murder, manslaughter, and driving offences.

Some prisoners may still be in the old IPP system (indeterminate imprisonment for public protection) which means they stay in prison until they can be released safely, while others have a fixed tariff (a specified number of years to serve) before parole is considered.

Since the Counselling Service at HMP X began, the sentence length of the prisoners that come here has been extended. When this change was put into effect, those serving less than four year sentences were transferred to other prisons. Only prisoners serving four or more years are now sent here.

Now that our clients are serving longer sentences, the work has changed. Demand is much higher and there is a significant increase in the childhood issues that are brought to our counsellors.

Anger is a common issue, fuelling crimes such as GBH (grievous bodily harm), ABH (actual bodily harm) and assault. Prisoners can feel the need to have their own way, and sometimes that requires the power of their fists to "prove" that they are right.

> L had been in-and-out of prison all of his adult life. His father had taught him that you must fight to get on in the world, and L applied that advice to every conflict he encountered.
>
> He was now back inside for the sixth time, serving a sentence of five years.

We worked on L's re-offending behaviour, identifying the old patterns that he slipped back into whenever he was released. The counselling service helped to give him the confidence to arrange to relocate upon his next release — leaving behind his old haunts, friends and temptations.

Learned behaviour from the past can also lead to knee-jerk aggressive reactions to authority figures and perceived threats. I have found that some of the prisoners who committed these kinds of crimes were reminded in some way of an abusive or bullying figure — they weren't hitting the victim but rather shadows from their past.

M had been beaten regularly by his uncle while growing-up. Years later, he had encountered a man who resembled his childhood abuser while out drinking with his mates.

When they argued, he lashed out — a scared and instinctive part of him convinced that he had to defend himself before he could be hurt again.

Many of the prisoners we see for counselling are first-timers. Often, their stories reveal ordinary lives which changed in an instant.

N was taking his girlfriend out for dinner when he lost control of the car. His girlfriend died instantly.

He had gone to the pub at lunchtime that day with his boss and had three pints.

N's life changed forever.

One night, O went out for a drink with friends to celebrate a deal at work. He didn't socialise much as a rule, preferring to spend time building up his business and being with his family. He needed persuading, but in the end enjoyed the change of pace and a couple of drinks with friends.

A noisy group of lads came in to the pub and started being disruptive nearby. Suddenly, a fight broke out and O and his friends were in the thick of it.

Within a few minutes, O's life changed. He was sentenced for a joint enterprise crime — liable not only for his actions during the fight, but also for the actions of his friends.

He was distraught — he had lost his business, his family, and his plans for the future. There was no point anymore. All because he had gone out for a drink with his mates.

P had had a hard day at work. He was angry and frustrated and needed some peace and quiet so he could think things through and work out what he needed to do. As soon as the door shut behind him, his partner started to argue with him.

He walked into the kitchen and found himself staring at the knife block as his partner went on and on. Within a few minutes, she was dead.

P cried throughout our early sessions, shame, regret and guilt pouring out of him. He loved his partner and couldn't understand what he had done.

It took a while for him to accept what he had done. Eventually he started the process of taking responsibility for his anger and understanding his habit of channelling that anger outward towards the people around him (a habit learned while surviving in the care system as a young boy).

Some prisoners are prolific offenders and they continue in their cycle of crime knowing nothing else.

Others arrive at a revelation: "I've had enough. I don't want to come back [to prison]."

The events and emotions that bring these men to the point of asking for help can be volcanic such as the death of a family member or the breakdown of a marriage.

Others take education courses during their time inside and find emotions unfolding as they invest in themselves, sometimes for the first time. They get chatting to the other students and sometimes share their story; afterward the tutor can recommend a referral to the Counselling Service.

Occasionally it is because nothing has happened; the weight of a structured life stacking-up day after day in neat layers can inspire heavy thoughts.

Q experienced two life changing moments.

One drunken night, he had lost control of his temper and his fists. A casual acquaintance revealed a connection with Q's childhood abuser and Q saw red.

Q came to counselling to talk about his anger and the links with his past. The work was going well and I felt sure that he would be able to process what had happened to him and his reactions on that night.

Then, I received a call out of the blue. Q had just found out that he hadn't been the only victim. His sister had revealed that she had also been abused during their terrible childhood. Q was inconsolable.

He felt he had let his sister down, that he had not been there for her. He felt that he had been a selfish teenager, only looking out for himself.

He cried uncontrollably while we talked. I was concerned about his emotional wellbeing so I told the officers about the state he was in and we organised some help for him. Forty-eight hours later he was finally coming out of the bubble of grief that had held him.

A week later he was back in counselling and talking about his relationship with his sister and the feelings of responsibility that dogged him. We talked about what he could and could not do as a young man — the restrictions that were out of his control.

Q has since become much closer to his sister, enjoying a strong and supportive relationship that would not have been possible if his anger had led to further criminal acts and time inside.

Q told me that he will never come back to prison, but that he had realised he had needed the experience to turn his life around.

> R lost his wife of 20 years to cancer. Afterwards, driven by grief and not caring what happened to him, he found himself out of control and in trouble with the police.
>
> He had no relatives, no friends.
>
> In prison, he plunged into despair. What did he have to live for? On release he would find himself alone again with £40 in his pocket and nowhere to be.

I listened, struggling to find the words for him. Sometimes all you can do is turn-up and show the client that someone is there for them in that moment. The work then begins in earnest in the next session.

Some clients have to grow up quickly to survive prison. They earn their maturity.

S was a young man, cocky and confident. He had learned that the only way to survive was to "show everyone who was boss."

He had a constant need to prove himself which led to countless arguments and fights.

One of these fights had led to prison.

When he first walked into the room I told him that counselling would only work if we were totally honest with each other. He sat down and burst into tears.

It was as though he had been waiting for the opportunity to let someone in.

His story poured out of him and suddenly I had a nine-year-old boy in front of me telling me about being bullied intensely at school.

At the end of that session we laughed and joked until he felt that he could face the other prisoners with his usual confidence. I opened the door and he swaggered out.

After another couple of sessions, I could see a change in him; he didn't need to show off any more. S left the prison shortly afterward and seemed ready to handle the world with a new maturity.

Sometimes the prospect of leaving prison can be the catalyst for an explosion of guilt.

T had been so excited to be driving his new car. He picked-up his partner and took her for a ride only to lose control going too fast around a bend. They hit a tree and his partner was killed outright. He was lucky to be alive but wished he had been the one to die.

Since then his life had been full of "If only ... ": If only he hadn't been driving; if only he hadn't been driving so fast.

Inside the counselling room, T was a frightened boy under immense pressure. Outside, he had to face the other prisoners and — when he was released — his family and the media.

His feelings of guilt and shame made him sick. T didn't want to live and as his release date approached, he felt worse and worse.

I found myself trying to build a boy back up to a man. A man who could understand and accept what he had done, and face the world outside the prison's door.

Chapter Summary: *Our Clients*

- The clients are varied in their backgrounds, crimes and personalities.

- Potential clients are assessed; fighting and other misdemeanours will suspend their referral.

- The service is not there for prisoners who just want some company.

- The stories we hear are humbling.

"If counselling is a vocation then counselling within the prison environment is a vocation within a vocation, not suited to everybody and certainly not for the faint-hearted."

A Counsellor

Five

Our Counsellors

To be a counsellor in prison, I believe you need to have a passion to do the best you can for a vulnerable person. But there's more.

Counselling in the prison is not about rehabilitation or fixing people. It's about listening and helping the client to move forward. It's not about your agenda or politics.

Counsellors at the prison must look beyond the word "criminal" and see the human being beneath. A high percentage of the clients we see are vulnerable men who are in prison because of problems rooted in their childhood.

You need to be able to see past the emotional chaos of the prison to be able to uncover the real story; opening your eyes to see the real person who's talking. Sometimes this means seeing the child within the adult, and then being willing to help the child find a way out of his turmoil.

Sometimes the stories are difficult to hear.

Counsellors at the prison must have a supportive, empathic manner and a great ear for the details that unlock each story.

> V had been repeatedly locked away in a cupboard when he was six-years-old because his parents had to go to work and thought the little boy would be safer left inside the small space.
>
> One night they forgot he was in there and the silent, obedient boy was left inside for 24 hours.
>
> Now 40-years-old, this big man is still terribly afraid of the dark.

The situations that are brought to the counsellors are intense, emotional and extremely personal and show how our learned behaviour from childhood affects us as adults.

When the client is vulnerable — as most of the prisoners are — It is important that they are "held" safely and securely and are not abandoned or rejected. Being genuine and honest is paramount.

If the clients in the prison were to experience the rejection of a counsellor — say if they were to leave the room, unable to cope with the session — all the past rejections of their lives return. It can be an upward battle to gain their confidence again and restart the counselling process.

Fitness to practise is incredibly important.

Over the years, I have seen the effects of tragedy and pain in the counsellors' lives. Despite trying to do their best, counsellors are only human. They take on clients with bereavement, relationship issues, anger, panic attacks or general anxiety. Sometimes their emotions become tangled with the clients'.

Explosions of anger or inappropriate sharing from well-meaning counsellors can still nevertheless spell the end of the placement.

Our own past must be locked-away. Only the client matters.

I imagine a doorway before every session; once I walk through it, I leave my problems behind. It's hard though.

When the client presents with abuse or a violent history, then the case is passed to a more senior counsellor. Most of the time we try to be aware of the possibility ahead of time, and ensure that we try and match clients with counsellors who have an appropriate level of proficiency and experience.

All clients are assessed before counselling starts to try to get a sense of what might come out. However, abuse doesn't always come out in these assessment sessions.

Trust comes hard for these clients so the counsellor must be able to deal with what is being expressed and see it through. The last thing the clients need is to experience more rejection from a counsellor who is not able to deal with their problem.

Working in the prison is unlike working with clients in other settings. We require counsellors in the prison to adopt a direct, integrative method that can be difficult for some, particularly those who are inexperienced or whose experience is based on classroom sessions.

Often, new counsellors start with a pre-conceived idea that they will be able to go into the session and leave the work to the client.

I was stopped by a prisoner one day while I was walking down the wing.

"When is my counselling going to begin?" he asked.

He told me that the person who came into the counselling room just sat there silently.

"I can't cope with that," he said, "I feel like she's judging me in her head."

The reality is that these clients live in an institution where they have become used to being told what to do, being challenged, and given direction. A counsellor who is sitting in a room silently is usually perceived as an intimidating presence and the client can become very uncomfortable very quickly.

The counsellors must also handle strong emotions inside the counselling room, and work to bring clients back down to a safe emotional place so they can walk back to their pad (room) and face the other prisoners again.

Then, they have to bear in mind that their client is locked inside a pad for hours at a time, with few distractions. He has all the time in the world to process what has been said in his counselling sessions.

Prisoners sit alone going over and over the same thoughts, feelings and memories, analysing what they did wrong and what was done to them. They can make connections and work through ideas quickly, or panic can set in and self-harm can offer a short-term release.

"Having a placement at the prison has been a unique experience. Clients often have very difficult and traumatic pasts, working with them to try and understand and make sense of how their past traumas are impacting and shaping their lives has been deeply rewarding.

The impact of having another person want to listen and be involved in their stories has been huge for them and also for me as a counsellor. There can be few other placements where it is so obvious that change can take place given the right conditions."

A Counsellor

Before we consider a counsellor to be settled, they must also demonstrate that they understand it is not appropriate to act on their own inside the prison.

Some come to the placement and think they know what to do in a crisis and they expect to just get on with it.

The rules are there for a reason though and the message is clear—there is a certain way of handling things in the prison and it is non-negotiable. The admin team are always there to provide support and guidance if the counsellors need it.

Counsellors in training can easily get stuck.

Inexperienced counsellors can become despondent and unable to get past obstacles in the therapy, and even experienced counsellors can become carried away by the emotions involved, refusing to accept that they have an issue until it's too late.

They believe they have experienced real issues in their peer role-playing during their courses, but this is not the same as seeing a live client. Real clients are not thinking about whether the counsellor is achieving their criteria. Or making sure the subject is not too unpleasant.

Real clients pour out their stories. It is fast and unpredictable and the counsellor can quickly feel overwhelmed.

In the prison, this usually happens during the second session with their first client. I think this first panic is an important milestone in the counsellor's development. The learning is huge if they are willing to admit to it.

During their interview process, and subsequent meetings and discussions, I try to prepare new volunteers for this early feeling. As a result, it is extremely rare that any counsellor ends their session early. Some remember their training; others freeze or panic but see it through somehow. They allow the client to keep talking until the end of the session, or move things to a more manageable place.

Afterward they say: "All I could think of was: 'What do I do next?'"

It is difficult to install confidence in newly qualified counsellors as they are often so completely wrapped-up in "getting it right."

There is no right answer in counselling. There is instead the ability to reflect, acknowledge, share and learn. Confidence can only be built with encouragement that whatever happens, it will be OK.

"What did you learn from it?" I ask new counsellors during supervision. This is the most important question.

"How will you deal with it if it comes up again?", is another important question.

It's OK for counsellors to make mistakes—as long as they learn from them. To feel that you know everything is arrogant and not useful in counselling.

Supervision is essential for identifying these problems.

Counsellors who have been working inside the prison for years often say that they started with a set of ideas that changed very quickly. Many of the counsellors I have worked with have blossomed during their tenure into caring, motivated and committed counsellors, gaining their accreditation along the way.

Recruiting new counsellors is difficult.

I advertise, contact colleges and universities, and use word-of-mouth. Still, the reality is that it is a volunteer job with no pay and no expenses.

In addition, the experience of being behind prison gates and walls is intense. When a hundred men are walking towards you on their way to another part of the prison, it can be scary.

> "I was with my client and suddenly there was shouting outside. My client reassured me that none of the prisoners would come in the room with us, and that an officer would pop by shortly. After a couple of minutes, sure enough one did. He asked if I was OK and then we just carried on."
>
> *A Counsellor*

Of course, there is also the reward of a fantastic experience that you couldn't get elsewhere.

Most of our volunteers have thrived and grown as counsellors during their time in the prison, and would agree that the experience was incredibly worthwhile.

There have been 60 volunteers who have passed through the gates since 2004, working from different theoretical backgrounds. Some stayed for a few months, some for five years.

Most of them say that the experience profoundly affected the counsellors they went on to become.

"At first, I was nervous. I worried about getting lost in the prison, about forgetting to lock the doors, about walking along cold corridors with prisoners walking past me. However, it took me only a few visits to become acclimatised and to actually start feeling more comfortable being there. The members of staff were marvellous and made me feel supported. I also enjoyed the good humour and the humanity on display amongst staff and prisoners alike. I enjoyed seeing my first clients, men who had never had therapy before despite living through lives marked by violence, disruption and low self-esteem.

The interesting thing for me is the challenge in building a therapeutic relationship within an enclosed setting, in building trust in prisoners who may be very suspicious of "authority." I am also privileged to hear about the challenges that these men have encountered and how they are coping (or not) with prison life. I think that providing therapy in prison is awesome."

A Counsellor

The Prison

(A poem from one of our counsellors)

Walking in through the doors
ID around your neck
Belt heavy on your waist
Electric doors controlled by officers
behind thick plastic screens
ID acknowledged
doors open, doors shut
Keys locked away behind more doors
attached to your belt
adding to the weight
Doors unlocked, doors locked
Footsteps echo along the corridor
waves of sound bounce back
murmurs, laughter, shouts
getting louder, getting closer
A crush of bodies heading towards you
but like the Red Sea
parts before it reaches you
Hello Miss, Hi Miss, like the hair Miss

Got any drugs Miss
words fired at you as they continue on their way,
off to work, off to gym
off to anywhere to fill the time.
In front of you they sit
the reasons they are inside are different
the reasons they are in front of you, the same
fear, anxiety, depression, anger
loneliness, bitterness, hopelessness
50 minutes to gain their trust
50 minutes for them to tell their story
50 minutes for them to see you don't judge them
50 minutes to start the relationship
50 minutes when they can be heard
not a number, a "perp", a criminal
a druggie, an offender, a murderer
Time is up, you part company
he to his pad, you back to the doors
Back through the corridors
empty of the bodies
quiet, apart from your footsteps
and shouts from behind closed doors
Through the security

the giving up of keys
doors open, doors shut
behind you
Out into the sun.

Fiona, A Counsellor

Chapter Summary: *Our Counsellors*

- Not every counsellor is suited for a placement at the prison.

- The experience of counselling in the prison can be overwhelming but very rewarding.

- It is particularly important that counsellors are able to leave their own issues at the door.

- Counsellors must be willing to observe the rules unquestioningly and to be totally honest at supervision sessions.

- Finding and recruiting new counsellors is challenging.

"As a counsellor, I am much clearer now about what interventions I use and why. I am more able to improvise because in a prison setting there may not be the materials that I would use in other placements."

A Counsellor

Six

Ways of Working

I have found in my experience as a counsellor in the prison that in many cases, a prisoner's crime starts from something that has happened in the past—something that has caused a young person to learn how to behave in a specific, possibly criminal way.

Much of what we do in our lives is because of learned behaviour. From the minute we come out of the womb, we learn when to cry, how to feed ourselves and how to interact with others. We learn how to read and write (sometimes) and we learn how to be part of the world. We continue learning all our life.

Many client's stories are heart-wrenching. They may have been abandoned at a young age, not wanted by those who should have cared for them, not good enough for those around them, and not loved by their family. A child can blame himself or herself very easily for this kind of loss; internalised feelings which build up over the years can turn into a volcano of anger.

Sometimes it's clear that prisoners were never taught how to interact successfully with the world, and never had a positive role model.

Children may be taught not to respect the authority figures in their lives by parents who themselves have little respect for teachers or the police. Children who live around crime may learn that stealing is an acceptable activity, perhaps even the only acceptable way to meet their needs.

In addition, peer pressure encourages vulnerable people to take drugs, isolating them further. In short order this can lead to desperation to feed their habit and stealing anything that can be sold.

Some prisoners have had a positive upbringing but then experienced trauma as an adult—such as bullying or becoming the victim of a crime.

By digging deep, exploring and questioning, our counsellors make links that enable the client to see where things went wrong, what they can take responsibility for and what wasn't their fault, and how they can change the pattern that keeps occurring.

W was 42 and he had never talked to anyone about his life because he was ashamed that the same patterns kept occurring. Together we looked at these patterns and where the trigger began.

His father used to beat him savagely every day. When he was 12, full of rage and hate toward his father, W ran away and vowed never to come back. He was caught and brought back home.

The beating he received landed him in hospital, and from there he was put into care. In care he suffered more abuse, although he felt it was an improvement on being with his father. He tried to make relationships with the other kids, but they broke up quickly when he lost his temper and lashed out.

His anger at his father had never stopped bubbling underneath everything he did.

Through counselling we explored his story, and slowly W could see results. He eventually became a mentor for other young men on the wing and began to work in the Education Department.

Once counselling begins in earnest, the counsellors use a toolkit of theoretical approaches which is guided by the needs of the client, not the counsellor's background or training.

During the initial assessment, we are in the here and now.

The client and counsellor discuss the boundaries of the arrangement and begin to look at why the client has asked for counselling, how they think it might benefit them, and at any current issues that they are dealing with (for example with visitors, family, health, etc.).

The counsellor may use Psychodynamic Theory to think about the client's past, and then work with them using elements of Cognitive Behavioural Therapy to change negative thoughts into positive.

Transactional Analysis may also prove useful when exploring the parent, adult and child aspects of the client's self and their relationships.

The loss of freedom that prisoners experience can produce an effect similar to the different stages of grief.

The realisation of a long sentence can be frightening as they think about what life will be like when they get out of prison. Prisoners serving very long sentences are faced with a very different world upon release.

Working within an existential framework to identify positives and find meaning in what's happened can help with any potential panic.

Sometimes we work with *Gestalt* ideas, encouraging clients to project to an empty chair, rehearsing and expressing emotion in a safe environment.

Visualisation is a very effective tool. Sometimes, this is about teaching clients to create a positive conclusion to their nightmare. At other times, it is about imagining a "safe place" that can provide an emotional sanctuary. Visualisation can distract a client from their anger or sadness, help them get to sleep, or tackle their fears head on.

Then, at the end of the session, the counsellor and client return to the here and now as the counsellor prepares the client to leave the room and go back out into the prison environment safely, all emotions packed away again.

At all times, we require the counsellors to maintain the core conditions of a person-centred approach.

In my private practice, I use all kinds of props to help my clients to tell their stories from pebbles, stones and buttons, to figures, toys and craft supplies.

In the prison, we are restricted from bringing anything in that a prisoner could pocket and use as a tool or weapon. They are so resourceful and inventive that we limit ourselves to paper tools and handouts only.

In particular, simple tools such as mind-maps and time-lines are frequently used.

I find that seeing words or drawings on a page can provoke genuine responses and help to organize chaotic memories. The physical act of creating an idea on paper gets that idea out of the client's head.

Some of the prisoners can't read or write, but there is always some way of representing their thoughts and feelings on paper.

In some cases, clients keep the finished handout on the wall in their pad as a reminder of where they are and where they are trying to get to.

One of my favourite tools is the Support Circle—clients can see at a glance all the people in their life; all the people who are waiting for them on the outside.

When X came to counselling, he said he had many areas in his life he wanted to talk about. We completed a mind-map, setting out all the issues and problems and people in his life.

"Wow," he said. "I have a lot in there that's stuck."

I asked him where he wanted to start.

When I met Y, he was very depressed. He believed there was no point — he hadn't done anything in his life except be a pain to everyone.

He said that he had nothing to feel proud of.

We drew a map showing all his achievements over the years, from his cycling certificate to the scouting badges that he gained as a boy, from the time he spent learning carpentry to his commitment in bringing up his children.

Y could see there was a lot of things that he had done. In-between sessions, he was able to look at the map and remind himself that he wasn't worthless.

Chapter Summary: *Ways of Working*

- Each client brings a different story and this requires a tailored, integrative way of working.

- Counselling focuses on helping the client to see things from a new perspective.

- Counsellors have to be creative as there are restrictions on what can be brought into prison.

"The counselling has enabled me to turn my life round and look to the future."

A Client

Seven

Historic Abuse

Abuse is a dark ghost in the lives of many of the prisoners. The details may change, and the severity of the mistreatment will vary, but the feelings of anger and betrayal, the need to escape, and the great bravery shown by those who finally tell of their secret abuse is similar.

And in nearly every case we can trace a contributory path from those painful secrets to the crimes these men have themselves committed. Being treated badly at the very point when they are learning about life affects how they come to view their place in the world and their perceptions of the boundaries of acceptable behaviour.

When role models are blurred or non-existent there is nothing to balance against these early lessons, and the abused child will grow in pain and anger into a pained and angry adult.

As Z sat there, rubbing his hands together, eyes on the floor, I knew there was more to come.

He had talked about his "non-existent" parents; about being put into care when he was four years old. About being abandoned and rejected because he wasn't good enough to stay in the family.

He had told me about the feelings he had had swimming around in his four-year-old head at that time.

"Why didn't they want me?" he had wondered. "Have I been naughty?"

His seven-year-old sister had gone to stay with Granny.

"Why can't I go to Granny's too? What's wrong with me?" he said, connecting vividly to his past.

"What do you remember about being in care?" I asked.

The silence stretched out between us for a long moment, and then tears began flowing down the cheeks of the grown man sitting before me. A moment later he was sobbing like a child.

Z was currently serving a sentence for GBH (grievous bodily harm) and the possession of drugs.

During our sessions, he bravely explored his thoughts and feelings — how he had internalised his anger, expressed it in needless fights which had resulted in him coming to prison numerous times, and taking drugs to escape his thoughts.

He had come to counselling because he felt he could not go on like this — he wanted to change. He wanted a normal life with his wife and children who were patiently waiting for him.

His story slowly took shape as we built a trust between us.

Z had been repeatedly abused while in care and had tried desperately to escape by running away. He would run whenever he got the chance, and try to get as far away as he could. But he was always bought back.

The abuse was continuous. It started as verbal and physical abuse when he didn't do what was asked of him, and then in his teens it became sexual.

I could see the shame and guilt Z felt weighing him down; these were his secrets and he couldn't tell anyone else.

In our work, Z slowly drew a mental picture of his abuser. First, a head that had no face, big shoulders and arms with huge hands in fists. A body full of muscles, huge thighs. But his boots were the thing that stood out—they were big and black with a steel toecap, and they were covered in my client's blood.

This picture took a few sessions to put together. Then the work began to help my client let go of each part of the abuser he remembered.

We created a new picture, talking about what this man could look like now. Z created a new mental image of a thin, weedy, unkempt, smelly man. A man not worthy of a single look.

I could see the difference in my client as he considered this picture. He stood taller as the man inside him let go of something that had been clenched tightly for so many years.

During our sessions, we had been putting together a time-line of his life. As we worked, we came finally to the event that was haunting him.

A had explained that drugs were a large part of his parents' lives. They were preoccupied and high much of the time. Against this backdrop, I could see how vulnerable A must have been.

The events of that long-ago evening had shaped his life. He believed he must be gay because of what had happened, and he believed that this was what relationships were like.

It took A weeks before he finally told me about an incident that had happened to him in his family home.

During those weeks, he had described many events in his life but had avoided the elephant in the room.

One day he arrived at our session in an agitated state. He started to tell his story — clearly desperate to get it out of his head and into the room. He had been thinking about it for days in his pad, and struggled to wait for our session once he had decided to tell it.

At 22-years-old, A had been groomed to be a "rent boy" and that life was all he had ever known. He was now in prison for ABH (actual bodily harm) and supplying drugs. During his time in prison he had been too scared to tell anyone about his past for fear that the other prisoners would find out and use the information to bully or assault him

Since being inside, he had become profoundly affected by the realisation that he had never been close to a woman in his life.

He told me about being alone in the house one evening, lying in bed, when a family friend came into his room and began to touch him. This man told him that what he was doing was OK and told him it was their secret.

We started painstakingly exploring his relationships and peeling back all the internalised feelings that A had been holding onto. My role was simple but very important—I had to listen and reflect so A knew I was right there with him as he told his story. I had to stay with him until the end.

Once the trust is there, the option to leave disappears.

A was angry that his life to that point had been influenced by the man who had abused him. He decided he wanted to talk to the authorities and we discussed the implications of going to court.

During this discussion, A told me that his abuser was to his knowledge working in a school.

This was a game changer for me. The rules that surround the counselling programme and my own practice dictated that I had to act.

First of all, I had to inform the appropriate person at the prison—this prisoner still had the choice whether to press charges against his abuser, but the school had to be given the information they needed in order to safeguard their students.

My second call was to my supervisor. I continued to talk to her at every step of the way about the implications of everything that was happening.

My client pressed charges against his abuser and gave the police a written statement. It turned out that the abuser had been abusing others. He was finally sent to prison himself, for a long time.

It didn't give A the closure he so desperately wanted, but he took some comfort in that no-one else could be hurt and affected the way he had been.

When B told me that he wanted to tell the police what his abuser had done, so that he could be prosecuted, we discussed the implications.

I wanted to make sure he knew that it is not straightforward. It's the same conversation I have with every client in this position.

We talked about the fact that others might be hurt, that the media might report the case and make it public. I made sure he understood that it is a big undertaking with many implications. I tried to prepare him for an unfavourable outcome — nothing is guaranteed.

B was still adamant

B and I had done some good work together, and now he felt that this was the next step to take.

He told me he was scared, and asked if I would sit in on the interview. I told him that would be fine as long as he understood that I wouldn't be able to say anything.

The police came to the prison and took all the details. They discussed the next steps with B and talked about what could happen next.

Later, my notes were used in his court case to show that he had told his story to me before going to the police. This is quite useful in these cases and can go some way to verifying what clients have said in their statements. The notes were copied by the prison with the client's permission and then sent to the Crown Prosecution Service (CPS).

I encourage all the counsellors to make proper detailed historical notes.

Some counsellors don't know how to write notes when they start at the prison, they have never been taught on their training. There is a myth that you shouldn't make notes and certainly not in front of the client.

This attitude can cause problems in the prison though.

C contacted the prison after his release. He was hopeful that he could use his counsellor's notes to corroborate his court case against his abuser, only to find that there was nothing available. His counsellor hadn't made a single note about his abuser.

This issue is now raised with new volunteers as soon as they start their placement. Detailed and complete notes are vital.

D had been involved in ritual abuse. He had been sexually abused by other family members and friends over a period of years.

He had kept it to himself until he came to counselling in HMP X.

A while after we had finished, he asked to see me again. He told me that he had received a letter from a family member who had taken their case of abuse to the police.

D was confused and didn't know what to do.

I talked at length with D, allowing him to explore his options and his feelings. He was still undecided when he left the prison a few months later.

Six months later, I was asked to produce my notes for court. He had found the courage to support the family member who had written to him.

Even though he had finished with the HMP X Counselling Service, and even though he had left the prison, his notes could still be used for this purpose.

Chapter Summary: *Historic Abuse*

- Many clients have been sexually abused as children.

- If their client is part of a court case, or wants to talk to the police about what happened to them, counsellors work within strict guidelines.

- Stories can be deeply upsetting; counsellors are supported during supervision and team meetings.

"It made me feel a better man
and my head is clear now."

A Client

Eight

Life Inside

When men first arrive in prison they are confronted with a lonely, isolating and scary reality.

Their new home is a small room with a bed in it and very little else. Their time is controlled. Their activities are controlled. The noises of the prison assault them: doors slamming, shouting, radios playing.

Some prisoners are particularly vulnerable and struggle to adapt. Counselling can help them to develop coping strategies to get through the nights, and the long, long days.

Sometimes prisoners fall out with each other. It stands to reason given the close confines. Sometimes it's because they don't get on with their pad-mate, or their pad-mate smokes or snores. There are many things which can cause anger and resentment.

We don't get involved in these arguments but it can affect the client's ability to focus on their counselling. Counsellors can find that their client just spends their time ranting about the cause of their upset. I tell the counsellors to listen for a few minutes and then take them back to the work they were doing.

E was doing well in counselling until one day the counsellor arrived to find that he was in the Segregation Unit. He had been in a fight over the weekend and mouthed-off to an officer. He was adjudicated (charged with a disciplinary offence) for not doing as he was told and ultimately transferred.

E had lost out again, all because he lost his temper, and now had to start again somewhere else. The counsellor felt the loss as well, and took this to supervision.

Sometimes prisoners express their struggle to cope through their hygiene. We see prisoners who have lost all respect for themselves, wanting to just give up and stay in their pad. They don't wash or shave, or want to change their clothes.

The prison regime doesn't allow prisoners to withdraw, however. Whether its education or work, they are encouraged to engage and try to improve themselves.

Officers also try hard with first-time prisoners to help them adjust to prison life, team them up with the right person or give them a friendly chat regarding keeping their pad clean and showering.

When they arrive for their first session, some prisoners will have made a special effort to shave and comb their hair. Others will appear quite scruffy. By the third session I usually find that those who had struggled at the beginning now appear smarter and more aware of their appearance. This is a good sign that they are starting to have a sense of pride in themselves.

Sometimes depression turns into something more dangerous.

Suicidal feelings can come from many sources. Perhaps a family member has died, or the prisoner has received a "Dear John" letter from a spouse or loved one ending their relationship. Sometimes it is simply the sound of their door shutting at 8 pm and knowing they have to spend the next ten hours alone.

When a client is first introduced to their counsellor, any existing warnings are highlighted. Sometimes an ACCT (Assessment, Care in Custody and Teamwork) has already been opened, and there is a plan in place to keep them safe.

If a counsellor becomes aware of new suicidal thoughts in a client, they have to report it. First of all, though, the counsellor discusses the plan with the client so they know what's going to happen next. Everything is transparent and the trust is maintained.

The counsellor informs the officers on the wing and arranges for an ACCT to be opened so the client continues to be supported after the end of the session.

Part of this is that the prisoner is checked on regularly and given the time and space to talk.

Mental health is high on the agenda in the prison. Many of the prisoners suffer from depression and other problems. It's not surprising when you find out how their lives began.

F told me that he had been put into care just for being the last child born to an over-stressed mother of five. He had defined himself as "unwanted" for the rest of his life.

Sometimes talking can help. Sometimes it doesn't. Sometimes all you can do is just let them "be", give them permission to feel the emotions that they are struggling with, and of course listen.

In addition to the staff in Healthcare, Mental Health, the officers, the counsellors, and other staff in the prison who can listen, there are the prisoners themselves. Listeners are volunteer prisoners who are trained and supported by the Samaritans. They are available 24/7 (round the clock) for prisoners in need.

Also, those prisoners who are recovering alcoholics can attend AA (Alcoholics Anonymous) meetings. These were introduced in 2005 after I had visited some AA groups on the outside and found out more about how they worked. The prison was receptive and, though numbers fluctuate, the meetings appear to provide a solid source of support for those prisoners who need it. The support continues on the outside when they leave.

Using the gym can help some prisoners find a constructive outlet for their anger. I've seen some over-use the gym to make themselves look bigger and stronger. In their minds that's their way of coping to beat the bullies or perpetrators.

G was a too-thin six-foot man who had been put down all his life. When I met him for the first time he wasn't eating properly or exercising.

Once he talked about his life and the physical abuse he had suffered by his dad, he slowly started to look after himself. As his story came out, his self-worth lifted and he stood even taller.

G began to use the gym regularly and became fit and toned — a different, more confident man greeted me at each session.

Six months later, I was walking down the corridor when I saw him again. Since our sessions had ended he had become very muscly indeed.

We talked about his relationship to the gym and his goals, and he revealed that his family had also noticed the change. He felt that it was going too far and wanted to find a balance. He was able to use the work we had already done to understand that he was viewing his body as a machine, and he needed to rediscover the man.

G was successful and subsequently became a mentor for new arrivals.

Prison life is deliberately busy and prisoners have lots of opportunities. They can plan for their release, improving their employability through taking courses in the Education Department or going to the workshops and learning a trade. Other courses may be mandatory for their sentence, such as victim awareness or relationship courses.

The Counselling Service tries to work around any of these activities so our clients don't miss out. I always encourage prisoners to try and do things they couldn't do when they were younger or didn't have the opportunities to do on the out.

There are many situations that can affect the counselling work in the prison, but we commit ourselves every time, and then deal with the unexpected when it happens.

Chapter Summary: *Life Inside*

- Life inside can be difficult.

- It can be hard for prisoners to maintain their self-esteem and personal hygiene.

- Coping strategies are varied.

- Procedures exist to monitor and protect vulnerable prisoners.

"I contacted my family because of the counselling and now I have contact with them after them pushing me away years ago.

I know where I belong."

A Client

Nine

The Outside

The outside can sometimes be a scary prospect when the institution is all that is known. Inside, prisoners can come to feel safe and secure.

H had no family waiting for him on the outside. The prison was his home now.

Counselling helped him to build confidence in himself, and look beyond the prison. He started helping others on his wing and became a mentor.

He began looking into all the places he could go to once he was on the outside and slowly became able to see a future for himself.

Loss is a major theme. The prisoners have lost their freedom as a result of their actions and this leads to so many more losses — job, home, family, and children.

Many prisoners get emotional letters and visits from their families in the early days of their stay in prison. Often, the message is supportive, but sometimes bombs are dropped.

Sometimes wives tell their husbands that they have had enough and want to end the marriage. They release the news during short visits where they have all the power and can simply walk away.

Sometimes fiancées explain in a letter that they have found someone else because they can't wait until the release date.

Understandable perhaps, but devastating for men who have been abandoned so many times before in their lives.

In the prison, we work with clients to explore their relationships. Sometimes there is a pattern of loss that can be linked to the attachments they made as a child.

J had custody of his children after his wife abandoned them. After four years of successfully holding his family together, he was persuaded by friends to go out one night and everything changed.

By the end of the evening he had been arrested for his involvement in a drunken bar fight.

His children were taken into care and his world fell apart.

The work we did in his counselling sessions enabled J to show social services that he could hold life together for his family. He left prison with a mountain to climb, but was more than willing to do it.

K's relationships with his family had broken down completely. His father was very angry with him for getting n trouble, as he had relied on him to inherit responsibilities in the family business.

A young man who had never taken his responsibilities seriously was now locked away from a family who needed him.

I helped K write a letter to his brother to make some amends and ask him to help the family cope while he served his sentence. Slowly he mapped out his future and tried to enlist others outside to help his family. He worked hard at communicating with them while he was in prison.

Eventually, his father came to visit and possibilities emerged for K's life after release. I watched him grow-up and become a more responsible man.

A lot of prisoners have children on the outside. Sometimes they are in contact with them; sometimes they don't know where they are. Sometimes they have a good relationship with the mother; sometimes it is bitter and difficult. Sometimes their children have no-one left to care for them and so they are fostered into the care system.

Occasionally, children reach an age where they can make decisions for themselves, and they seek contact with their father again.

All too often, the children gradually fade from their lives, pulled further and further away by the reality of the sentence that dad is serving.

For many prisoners, the loss of their children is a crushing blow. We encourage these fathers to work hard at bettering themselves, so their partners and children can see that they are trying to change.

Where possible, the prisoners at the prison cling onto their children with photos and letters. There is a wonderful scheme at HMP X whereby prisoners can read aloud a story onto tape to be sent home, so the child can hear their voice.

We tell them that even though they may not receive a reply, it still means something to try and stay in contact. And there is always the chance that one day their letters will be read.

L was seven when he lost his dad and sister to a house fire. His mum was devastated and sent him away to live with his Gran.

After some angry outbursts, his Gran had to admit that she couldn't cope and he was put into care.

L grew from an angry young man to an angry adult who was often in the middle of a fight. Eventually he got married and had two kids, but his wife left after L's anger pushed her away.

When I saw him, he was in prison for possession and couldn't see any way forward.

We slowly worked to identify what had been lost, and what could be saved if he worked on himself and his anger.

Six months later, L had started an education course and had been in contact with his Gran who was helping him get in touch with his children. He could see a future.

Chapter Summary: *The Outside*

- The outside world can be a source of shattering news and change.

- Family is important in helping prisoners cope with life inside and outside.

- Counsellors work to re-establish family links where possible.

Afterword
Looking Ahead

After nearly 17 years of being involved with the Counselling Service, I feel an enormous sense of achievement.

Throughout that time, I have seen many changes in the prison regime, but the men who have come to the service for help have remained the same — focused on rebuilding their lives and facing up to their pasts.

Sixty counsellors have also come and gone in that time, their enthusiasm and their subsequent growth as professionals a great source of pride.

Our service is unusual among other prisons for being embedded within the prison structure. By taking this approach we have been able to address issues of confidentiality, security and accountability with a degree of control and specialist supervision that other prisons operating agency models can't match.

I have made mistakes along the way. Setting up a counselling service in such a unique environment is fraught with potential pitfalls. I have offered placements to counsellors who proved to be entirely unsuited to the structure we have to adhere to and the atmosphere we have to work within. I have also discovered new applications of confidentiality and new tests for the ethics of my profession.

I have also been touched by the courage of my clients. Their willingness to look unflinchingly at themselves and their actions has been an inspiration.

I would like to see more prisons take a step toward owning their own counselling service, and I would also like to think that counsellors could be valued in those services with some contribution toward their expenses or provision for a small fee. Finding counsellors who are in a suitable position to work voluntarily is difficult.

I don't know what the future will bring for the Counselling Service at HMP X. I don't know how the attitudes in this country and within our government will change regarding the value and desirability of providing counselling to those who have broken our laws. I do know from my own experience that counselling works to effect change.

Counselling is listening, and the men in UK prisons are desperate to tell their stories.

Further Reading

An Introduction to Counselling, John McLeod, Fifth edn, 2013 (Open University Press)

Counselling for Toads: A Psychological Adventure, Robert de Board, 1998 (Routledge)

On Becoming a Person: A Therapists View of Psychotherapy, Carl R Rogers, New edn, 2004 (Robinson)

Overcoming Anger and Irritability: A Self-help Guide Using Cognitive Behavioral Techniques, 2009, William Davies (Robinson)

Counselling Survivors of Childhood Sexual Abuse, Claire Draucker and Donna Martsolf, Third edn, 2006 (SAGE Publications Ltd)

Games People Play: The Psychology of Human Relationships, Eric Berne, Reprint Edn, 2010 (Penguin)

Overcoming Depression: A Self-help Guide Using Cognitive Behavioural Techniques, Paul Gilbert, 2009 (Robinson)

Criminal Justice: An Introduction to the Criminal Justice System in England and Wales, Malcolm Davies, Hazel Croall and Jane Tyrer, Third Edn, 2005 (Longman)

Suicide in Prisons: Prisoners' Lives Matter, Graham Towl and David Crighton, 2017 (Waterside Press)

Interventions in Criminal Justice: A Textbook for Working in the Criminal Justice System, Peter Jones, 2012 (Pavilion Publishing and Media Ltd)

Interventions in Criminal Justice: A Handbook for Counsellors and Therapists Working in the Criminal Justice System, Vol. 2, 2015, Peter Jones (Pavilion Publishing and Media Ltd).

Index

Transgender Behind Prison Walls
by Sarah Jane Baker
With a Foreword by Pam Stockwell

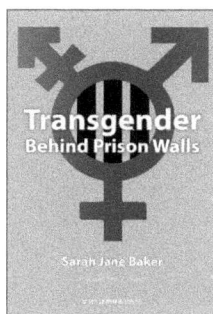

After explaining 'What is transgender?' this first book on transgender
in a prison setting looks at the entire HM Prison Service regime for
such people. Ranging from hard information about rules and regula-
tions, the transition process and how to access it to practical suggestions
about clothing, wigs and hairpieces, make-up and coming out, the
book also deals with such matters as change of name, gender identity
clinics, hormones, medication and use of prison showers and toilets.

'An important contribution to current debates on the treatment
of transgender prisoners'— Mia Harris, Oxford University.

Paperback & ebook | ISBN 978-1-909976-45-0 | 2017 | 160 pages

www.WatersidePress.co.uk

The Little Book of Prison

A Beginners Guide

by Frankie Owens

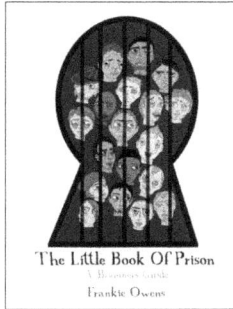

The Little Book Of Prison
A Beginners Guide
Frankie Owens

An easy-to-read prison survival guide of do's and don'ts. Perfect for anyone facing trial for an offence that may lead to imprisonment, their families and friends. Packed with humour as well as more serious items. Backed by prisoner support organizations. Straightforward and highly entertaining.

'By the end of the book, I felt like Frankie Owens was my cell-mate. His style and execution is either perversely skilful or an absolute fluke, but whatever it is, it is certainly good'— *Prison Service Journal*

'A fun, easy to read little guide to the bits of prison life they never tell you about at induction'— *Inside Time*

Paperback & ebook | ISBN 978-1-904380-83-2 | 2012 | 112 pages

www.WatersidePress.co.uk

Suicide in Prisons

Prisoners' Lives Matter

by Graham Towl and David Crighton

With a Foreword by Lord Toby Harris

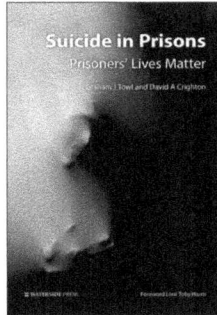

The definitive guide from two leading authors central to developments in the field. An invaluable book which covers everything from theoretical and community research to precisely what is known about prisoners and the risk of their completing suicide. Covers the Harris Review and Government Response to it as well as the stance of politicians, reform groups and other leading experts on what is an escalating problem for UK prisons. Contains analysis and data from over 30 years, bringing together key knowledge and information at a critical time of concern and attention.

'Makes for uncomfortable but essential reading for all those responsible for the policy and practice of suicide prevention'— John Podmore, Prisons Consultant and former prison Governor.

Paperback & ebook | ISBN 978-1-909976-44-3 | 2017 | 208 pages